7. 6,219
    × 3

11. 48,061
    × 7

15. $280.07
    × 9

19. 43,663
    × 6

23. 27,006
    × 3

8. 8,704
    × 4

12. 68,314
    × 8

16. $328.24
    × 8

20. 96,459
    × 7

24. $860.10
    × 6

Work Space

$25.50
×   4

Answer ___ $297.28

3. There were 14 boys and 16 girls in the class. The room had 25 desks. How many more desks were needed?

Answer ___ 5 desks

4. Terri had saved $30. She then spent $2.98 for a game and $7.85 for a blouse. How much does she have left?

Answer ___ $19.17

5. Terry had $10.50. He spent $5.85. He then earned $7.75 more. How much does he have now?

Answer ___ $12.40

6. Angela bought 4 cakes for $0.85 each and 2 cans of juice for $0.79 each. How much did she have to pay?

Answer ___ $4.98

7. On Saturday, Marty worked 8 hours at $7.00 per hour and 3 more hours at $10.50 per hour. How much did he earn?

Answer ___ $31.50

Holt, Rinehart and Winston, Publishers   Workbook 352   HOLT MATHEMATICS

To my family, friends
and anyone who has ever experienced the joy of a child.
–Marilyn Adams

To Keith, forever young,
and to Ari, young only once.
–Paul Micich

Special thanks go to the many people who
educated us about the universal stages of
grief — and recovery, via professional or
personal insights, and thereby helped
expand the message of this book.

Foreword

My whole professional life has been devoted to the surgical problems of children. As many as the challenges were, trauma was one of the most demanding. With children most of the injuries are unintentional and we usually call them "accidents."

The term "accident" gives those around a child a sense of comfort— for, after all, an accident is nobody's fault. Yet unintentional injury is largely avoidable and therefore preventable. That was the founding principle behind the National SAFE KIDS campaign which I have chaired for seven years. This is a grassroots campaign with more than 200 coalitions in every state of the Union. The mortality for unintentional injury in this country has fallen by 14 percent in seven years.

The attractions that lead to unintentional injury vary from region to region in the country. Kids don't fall through thin ice on ponds in the Southwest. Nor are swimming-pool drownings as common in the North as they are in warmer parts of the country. Marilyn Adams opened my eyes to the fact that in rural America, farm life presents a unique set of booby traps for youngsters that can lead to unintentional injury and, sadly, even death, including her own son's.

Because of that death, Marilyn Adams founded Farm Safety 4 Just Kids and has alerted those of us who are injury-sensitive to the unique pitfalls that exist for youngsters on farms.

Another way I resonate with Marilyn Adams is over the loss of her son. My wife's and my 20-year-old son died on the brink of manhood in a mountain-climbing "accident" in which the face of the cliff peeled off and carried him with it. Marilyn, not being in any way maudlin, makes the reader understand her pain and her slowness of recovery, but emphasizes the essential ingredient of hope.

It is always sad that a contribution such as this book comes through tragedy, but we are all better off when understanding the author's grief, innovativeness, drive and courage.

– C. Everett Koop, M.D., Sc.D.
Former U.S. Surgeon General

A VOICE FOR RURAL CHILDREN

Marilyn Adams
Spokesperson, President, and Founder
Child Farm Safety Advocate

Farm Safety 4 Just Kids

1-800-423-KIDS

PO Box 458 • Earlham, IA 50072 • www.fs4jk.org
email: marilyna@netins.net

iction

to you by others.
e embrace of a friend
f a stranger.

ve to yourself. But only
ne is right.
ready to begin to heal.

iences profound loss,
n to me at first.

t associated with your own life.
xperience, and denying that does

at no parent can bear to imagine.
o have lost someone — or
ever again living without pain
g fulfilled, laughing or loving.
er come, or that hope would

ine. I have been given back my life
my story.

er profound loss, and help those

Rhythm of the Seasons

A journey beyond loss

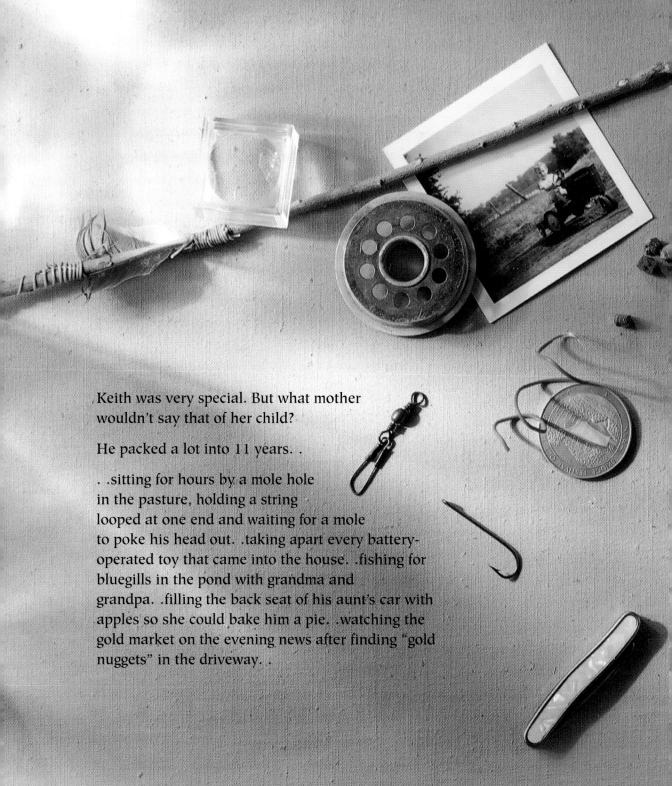

Keith was very special. But what mother wouldn't say that of her child?

He packed a lot into 11 years. .

. .sitting for hours by a mole hole in the pasture, holding a string looped at one end and waiting for a mole to poke his head out. .taking apart every battery-operated toy that came into the house. .fishing for bluegills in the pond with grandma and grandpa. .filling the back seat of his aunt's car with apples so she could bake him a pie. .watching the gold market on the evening news after finding "gold nuggets" in the driveway. .

. . camping in the back of an old, weathered pick-
up. .planting saplings out back with Darrell, his
stepfather. .

He lived with the abandon and
sheer joy only a child knows.
It was a joy he shared with
those who loved him.

5

The memories unravel into familiar stories. One, now, is particularly precious.

It was our last Sunday together. Darrell had to get ready for harvest, so Keith became the self-appointed dad when it was time to go to church. He said I looked nice and smelled good. He reminded his sisters and me to buckle our seat belts. He led us to our pew. Third row from the front on the left-hand side. The girls and I had to slide in first so he'd be on the end. When it was time for the offering, I slipped him some change. But he gave it to his sister, Kim, then took a dollar out of his pocket. He pulled the bill on both ends, so it made a popping sound, held it up to his lips and kissed it good-bye. As he laid it in the plate, he was grinning from ear to ear.

I could not have known then
how precious that moment would become.

Nor how soon.

Harvest began the following Tuesday. As always,
Keith rode his bike to the barnyard to help his stepfather
as soon as he got home from school.

The process was simple.
Darrell ran the combine — a
10-ton machine that gobbles
up six rows of corn at a time,
removes the kernels, and
spews cobs and husks in its
wake. He would fill a gravity-
flow wagon with the kernels,
pull the wagon into the
barnyard, park it next to the
auger and return to the field.

Keith ran the auger, a 60-foot
corkscrew that catches the kernels
as they flow out the wagon's side
door. As the giant corkscrew turns,
it carries the kernels up into the
storage bin. All Keith had to do was
turn on the auger, using power
supplied by the barnyard tractor.

Once the wagon was empty, he would shut off the power, then stand on the wagon's ladder, watching and waiting for the next load.

There is a rhythm here. One picks the corn from its plant.
The other puts the corn away. Pick. Put away. Pick. Put away.

The rhythm of the harvest is the rhythm of our lives.

It was evening when Darrell mentioned he'd like Keith to stay home the next day and work. Something about the suggestion bothered me, but I'd known it was coming. Staying home to help harvest is a rite of passage. It's an 11-year-old trading a day of school for a taste of his future on the farm.

As we talked it over in the barnyard, the chill of autumn pushed us closer together. "Well, young man," I said to Keith, "I guess you have a big day tomorrow! You'd better get to bed!" Keith tried to look serious, but it didn't work. Instead, he grinned all the way to the house, the beam from his flashlight bobbing back and forth, in sync with his gait.

I watch him and, once again,
my heart seems to burst with love.

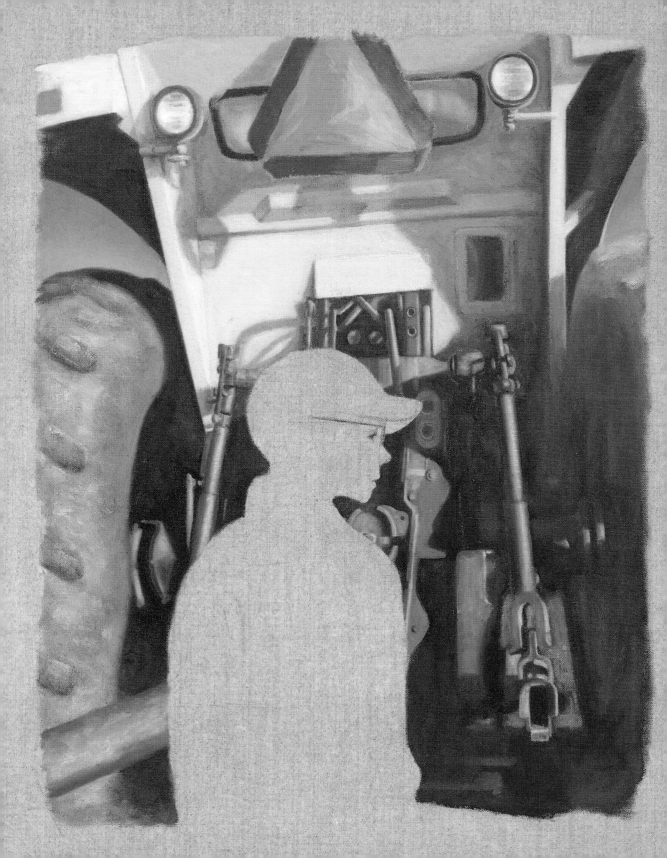

Harvest morning, with the sky between darkness and dawn, was crisp, exhilarating. The weather would be perfect. Farmers can feel it in their bones.

I had to leave for a job-required computer refresher class in the city. As I passed our breakfast table, an uneasiness stirred within me. I wanted to lecture Keith about safety. Instead, I kissed him good-bye. "You be careful, okay? Mom loves you!"

Keith kept popping into my mind that morning. I knew he'd be alone in the barnyard most of the day and the notion made me feel uneasy. I pictured Darrell pulling into the barnyard every half hour with a wagon load of corn, waving to Keith waiting on the ladder, heading back to the field, and waving again over his shoulder as Keith turned on the power for the auger. I could almost sense the rhythm of their work, but I could not concentrate on mine.

Just before noon, I thought about calling Grandma Adams. I could reach her before she took lunch to the barnyard. I'd ask her to remind Keith to be careful. But then, he always was careful. So I didn't call. I ran an errand instead.

At 3 o' clock, I felt their rythym break.

In each of us, there is an inner voice. Although we don't know where it comes from, it is a part of us, even before we understand the need for it.

"Marilyn?" It was the receptionist, tapping me on the shoulder. "You have a phone call."

"Marilyn, this is Julie from the clinic in town. Your son's been hurt."

*yourson
hurt*

*youholdontothephone
butyouhearnothing
youstareahead
butyouseenothing
rawterrorstrikesateveryfiberofyourbeing
icerunsthroughyourveins*

youcanneithercomprehendnormove

youcanonlyscream NO-O-O-O

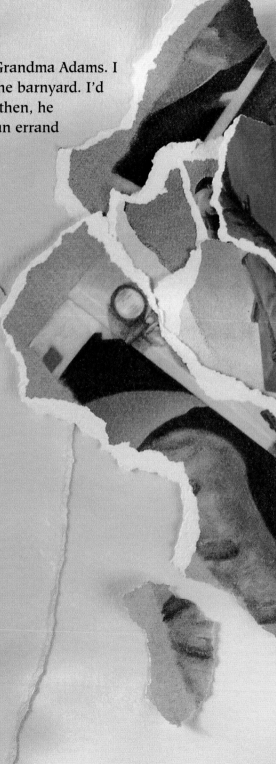

Two people drove me to the hospital. The entire time, I asked questions they could not answer. "What could have hurt Keith?" "Did he get a bump on the head?" "Why are you driving so slowly?" "Everything will be all right, won't it?"

A chaplain met us in the emergency room, saying only, "Your son was air-lifted here. They're working on him now." Darrell arrived within minutes, looking dirty and aged. His face was ashen and tear-streaked; his eyes mirrored the horror I felt growing inside me. We stood before one another for a moment, until our unrelenting sobs broke the silence.

Slowly, I pieced the afternoon together. Darrell had turned into the barnyard and sensed trouble immediately. Keith wasn't standing on the ladder's rung, waiting. The auger was running but corn was only trickling out the wagon's side door. Something was blocking the flow. Even before he saw Keith's leg in the side door, Darrell knew.

". .I was like a crazy man, grabbing at Keith's leg and foot. .wouldn't come out. .too much corn. .finally turned the wheel on the side door to widen the opening. ."

As Darrell inched the door upward, 14,000 pounds of corn began to pour over Keith and out the door. He grabbed again at Keith's leg and foot, but the weight of the corn still in the wagon had a far stronger hold.

". .it was like a blizzard of corn. .dust everywhere. I could see Keith. .fetal position. .pulled and pulled, but I couldn't get him out until the wagon emptied." Darrell paused, then looked at me squarely. "I killed him, Marilyn! He's dead!"

"No, Darrell! No! What's going on? He's not dead! Keith's alive! Our Keith is alive! They're working on him! The chaplain told me so!"

Darrell grabbed me by the shoulders. "Marilyn, he had to have suffocated in the corn. I tried to blow into his mouth. .tried to dig the corn out of his throat. .oh, God, I tried."

I could not respond. I, too, was suffocating.

In Kahlil Gibran's The Prophet *it is written that your child comes through you but is not from you. There are times, however, when* The Prophet *is wrong. There are times when your child is from you. There are times when your child is you.*

My mind could only grasp bits and pieces of that night.

Someone dressed in white took us to Keith. Amidst all the doctors and nurses, our little boy lay motionless on a gurney, hooked up to everything, an oxygen mask covering his dirty — now tiny — face. Someone else in white called to us, "Tell Keith to breathe. You never know when the patient can hear you."

In intensive care, they had put screws in his head to monitor brain swelling. His eyes and lips were puffy, his skin purple and his face a blotchy red. "Keith," I whispered, "we have to talk to Jesus now." Praying was appropriate. Keith was going to be a minister when he grew up. He'd said that for years. As I murmured prayers, a tear formed in the corner of his eye, and slowly rolled down his cheek.

Darrell stood back, against the wall, staring ahead vacantly, and then, ". .too young to work alone. .should have been in school. .should have done it myself. ."

Soon after that, a nurse came in to offer him an empty bed. "Go," I said. "Rest awhile." We held each other for a moment, so drained that we were limp. Then, he shuffled after her, shoulders slumped, head down. I don't think he knew where he was going. Nor did it seem to matter. The weight of guilt was crushing him.

From then on, my mother and I kept a silent vigil. Deep in the night, Keith's uncontrollable trembling caused by shock began to subside. I leaned over him, my hands covering his, my eyes searching his face, my prayers providing a blanket for his body. And then, at last, the trembling gave way to stillness and peace. I glanced up at the clock. It was 2:30 a.m. The monitors continued to blink, but my heart told me they no longer served any purpose.

Brain wave tests later that morning confirmed what I knew. Organ donation papers were signed. I remember saying good-bye, not believing my own words, not recognizing the sound of my own voice.

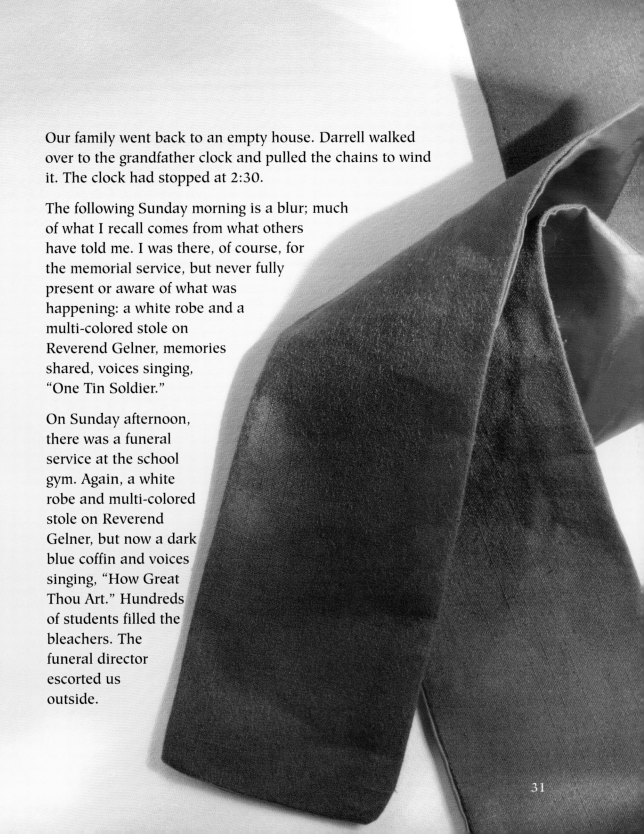

Our family went back to an empty house. Darrell walked over to the grandfather clock and pulled the chains to wind it. The clock had stopped at 2:30.

The following Sunday morning is a blur; much of what I recall comes from what others have told me. I was there, of course, for the memorial service, but never fully present or aware of what was happening: a white robe and a multi-colored stole on Reverend Gelner, memories shared, voices singing, "One Tin Soldier."

On Sunday afternoon, there was a funeral service at the school gym. Again, a white robe and multi-colored stole on Reverend Gelner, but now a dark blue coffin and voices singing, "How Great Thou Art." Hundreds of students filled the bleachers. The funeral director escorted us outside.

Finally, the cemetery. People everywhere. Clouds moving in circles. Are my feet on the ground? I press on my temples but the throbbing doesn't cease. I know where I am, but all the pieces of my life seem scattered: in the clouds, among the people gathered to sing and pray, and there, in the ground, where Keith's coffin will be lowered.

It would be a long time, many seasons, before the pieces of my life would come back together, before I would feel whole again.

I staggered aimlessly through that first year, so numb I couldn't think, exhausted but unable to sleep. Some days I was detached from reality; other days, shocked by it. I ached with emptiness, my body bent over with sorrow.

Looking back now, I realize I was beginning to venture into the maze of grief: denial, anger, bargaining, depression, acceptance. But I didn't move neatly from one stage to the next. No, nothing was that easy; no progress could be charted. Instead, I might slip from one emotion into another, or be jerked there mercilessly. Back and forth I'd go. Over and over again.

I did not realize that the journey
to acceptance was complex, gradual and difficult.

I did not even realize that acceptance was possible.

But it is.

I knew the rest of that autumn would be difficult. It is, after all, a season of evening, with fields cleared and early darkness drawing families together in the comfort of home.

But we did not come together. Darrell buried himself in farming. He was busier than usual, more quiet than ever. The girls went back to school and appeared to find peace in familiarity. In the evenings, Darrell and Kim would say little about Keith; Kelly would cry openly. Then, the three of them would be pulled together by a common task — preparing dinner, perhaps, or doing homework. I realized that Darrell was becoming mother to Kelly and Kim. And the girls were becoming caregivers to both me and their father.

I was neither wife nor mother, only observer. I watched them get on with their lives. Watched them reach out to me, but I could not feel their touch. Instead, I spent my time pleading with God to let Keith slide into our pew. I'd scold Keith, saying, "You've always done everything I told you to do. Now, it's time for you to come home."

I even wondered how Darrell could let this happen to "my" son.

On bearable days, I counted each hour. On unbearable days, I counted each minute. I waited for nighttime. And when it came, I found no reason for having lived through the day.

Parades of people came by. Again, I only observed them. Until one Saturday when my friend Jenny stopped in. We settled by the fireplace, drinking hot cider. Jenny didn't say, "I know how you feel. ." (because she couldn't know). Instead, she listened. And finally, Jenny held me and we cried.

I knew winter would be difficult. It is, after all, a silent season of barren fields, gray skies and snow falling on Christmas morning.

The holidays were excruciating. One afternoon as we went through the motions of Christmas shopping, I stopped by a tree in a department store. It was covered with ornaments, each bearing the name and age of a needy child. I took one off and bought a robot for an 11-year-old boy.

Our extended families gathered, talking and, somehow, laughing as meals were shared and stories told. As I watched them reestablishing their lives, I could feel the hollowness inside me pushing outward as though I were a balloon that soon would explode. A comforting thought. Some days, it was more painful than a physical hurt. I wept for the snow angels that used to be in the front yard.

I knew spring would be difficult. It is, after all, a time to shed the long, dark days of winter for warmth and light. To turn the earth and plant the future. To hope.

Mistakenly, I thought my painful firsts were over — Thanksgiving, Christmas, Valentine's Day, Keith's birthday. Since we'd been going to church regularly, I hadn't anticipated that Easter would be so bad. But perhaps Easter was the worst in a year of "firsts" because of the message of the season — that God gave up His only son to death. A death followed by a resurrection.

That Easter Sunday, I had no little minister sitting by me in the pew. I'd experienced the death. But not the resurrection.

I loved Keith too much. That was it! At times it seemed that I loved him way more than the girls or Darrell loved him.

Darrell.

How could he have let this happen? How could he get through each day? Why didn't he ever talk about Keith? Why didn't he hold me when I cried? "You weren't a good father to him." My words flew out like shrapnel. "You didn't have time for him. Didn't play catch or do fun things with him. You were — you are — a workaholic." My accusations hung in the air, then shattered over Darrell like broken glass.

He did not deny my words. Instead, he grew cold and I responded in kind.

"Only 10 percent of the marriages survive the loss of a child," the counselor told me. "Never lose sight of how important your family and marriage are. You need to stick together now. You need each other. You, Darrell, both of your families. All of you have already lost too much. It takes work to keep everything together because grief and stress can play tricks with your mind."

Yes, tricks. Sometimes I'd end up behind the school bus on my way to work. I'd look at the kids peering out the window and know that Keith's face was going to appear. When it didn't, once again despair filled my life.

I knew summer would be difficult. It is, after all, a time when young men work with their fathers, learning the trade. A time for little men and crops to grow.

At the very least, I had hoped by now that the physical pains would diminish. The throbbing headaches, piercing stomach cramps, aching all over. That was not to be.

As well, I could only continue to watch my family moving forward. I think they still reached out to me. Maybe not. I felt no touch. Slowly, I was concluding that they could survive without me. The counselor was right; it would take a lot of work to keep us together. Too much work. I found it curative to conjure up ways to die. The scenarios came easy. .

I'd stop the car on the railroad tracks and wait for the train. But what if I only got injured? They'd say I was insane and take my kids away.

I'd leave the car running in the garage. But what if the girls found me? I couldn't do that to them.

In desperation, I went back to the counselor, my words spilling out. "I can't live without Keith. If I die, I can see him again. I'm not even a good mother anymore."

"Marilyn," the counselor responded, "just make sure you stop, regroup and don't follow through with any of those notions. Even though it seems difficult to believe, you will begin to make choices that bring you happiness again. You will find purpose in life once more. Let others help you heal."

". .happiness. .purpose. .healing. ." Soothing words. I was weary of being angry and not caring. I was sick of being depressed and sad. I was tired of being tired. For the first time in almost a year, I let myself think about such comforting promises.

Could, indeed, there be change?

Life is about choices.
No matter what you have lost,
you still make choices.

As the first year stretched into the second, I began to realize that my life was no longer about what I wanted, because what I wanted most, I could not have. Rather, my life was about living with what I had. And the challenge, then, became choice — that is, choosing from what is offered because you can't choose from what cannot be.

Gradually, I chose to think about the Keith I had before his death because those memories were happy. I'd see him picking me another bouquet of daisies. I'd visualize us sitting on the pick-up tailgate, wishing upon the same star. I'd remember how he teased his sisters and planted trees with his step-dad.

His sisters. His Dad. They'd been waiting for me, sometimes patiently, other times not. Kim and Darrell had grieved for Keith, though not openly, the way Kelly and I did, the way I thought grieving should be. Consequently, I hadn't understood that they were grieving, too. I realized that I missed them — all three of them — and ever so slowly, I began choosing to rejoin my family.

Life is about choices, and choices can help you find purpose.

There is a time for every thing, and for every purpose.

In small ways, I was taking control of my life again. But for what? I was looking for a purpose, something to think about besides my loss. Still, as is often the case, when that purpose came along, I didn't recognize it.

It was Kelly who mapped out my journey. Now a high school senior, she was preparing a presentation about Keith. "I need your help, Mom," she said. "I have to get some facts about gravity flow wagons." Her request struck at that hollow spot still inside me, but I couldn't tell her no. So we contacted manufacturers of gravity flow wagons and found that they provided no warning labels or safety information to customers about suffocation. One evening, Darrell joined our discussion. "Maybe I can create something that will show the problem," he offered. He filled a toy wagon with unpopped popcorn, placed a toy person on the top of the corn and opened the side door. Within seconds, the toy person was buried.

As I watched Darrell's experiment, I felt that familiar heartache. I looked up at Darrell, then at the girls, and saw that same misery in their eyes. We were missing Keith together. As a family. By the time I climbed into bed, the sorrow had transformed itself into a mother's concern — not for herself but for those around her. I looked over at Darrell and, somehow, I knew he harbored that same concern.

I still did not know, though, that the seeds of purpose had been planted.

Hope is a gift we receive from others.
And it is from hope that healing emerges.

No matter how great your loss, others can help you heal.

Kelly's presentation to our state's Future Farmers of America organization received high honors and eventually caught the attention of state and national figures in the farm safety and health movement. Within a year, the need for farm safety precautions ignited so much interest that we established a non-profit organization. I named it **Farm Safety 4 Just Kids**, because the ones who were dying were just kids. Through the project, I began to merge with others — friends and strangers — were approaching. By permitting me to connect with their lives they enabled my own to blossom.

Like the woman who called my office pleading. "I need to see you. .talk to you. .my son died while helping his dad. .can't cope. .live an hour away. .don't care that the weather is awful. .please, can I meet with you!" As we sat and talked, I saw the agony of my own loss reflected in her eyes. So I told her that I understood how she felt, and she knew that to be true. I had helped her. And she had helped me.

Like the stranger who sat next to me on the plane. "My mother died recently," he said. "We were so close, but as a doctor, I deal with death all the time. .never dreamed hers would be this hard. .can't seem to handle it. .get depressed. .then angry. .emotions all over the place. .guess you understand, right?" And we who began the journey as strangers ended it as friends, feeling each other's loss, carrying each other's grief.

Like the friend whose son had cancer. "I'm devastated. I get up from the dinner table, go into the bathroom and cry. Just like you used to do after Keith died. I remember watching you. Hearing how you couldn't take care of the girls. .couldn't relate to Darrell. .It's happening to me. .What can I do. .Please!" As we sat and talked, I neither judged her nor tried to solve her problem (because I couldn't). When she left, again I felt stronger because I had shared my experience.

I was beginning to feel the hollow spot fill as the missing pieces slowly came back to me.

But it was in the night when the gift of hope became the reality of healing. When I couldn't sleep, I'd go into the living room and read Keith's Bible. One night, I came across James 3:13; my little minister-to-be had drawn a box around the passage:

"Is there anyone among you who is wise and understanding? He is to prove it by his good life, by his good deed performed with humility and wisdom."

Interesting passage. One, obviously, that had been important to Keith. I wanted to ask somebody about a connection between the "good deed" and **Farm Safety 4 Just Kids**. But everyone was asleep. The notion struck me that I would like to ask Keith, but I realized I already knew his answer.

And as I drifted off to sleep, I felt almost whole once more.

You can make choices.
You can discover purpose.
You can receive the gift of hope.
You can begin to heal.

But you cannot have what cannot be.

There was a time when I was concerned merely with surviving. But as I slowly regained my life, that fear faded. In its place, there emerged an awareness that while you can never get over profound loss, you can learn to live with it.

And finally, acceptance slips quietly into your soul.

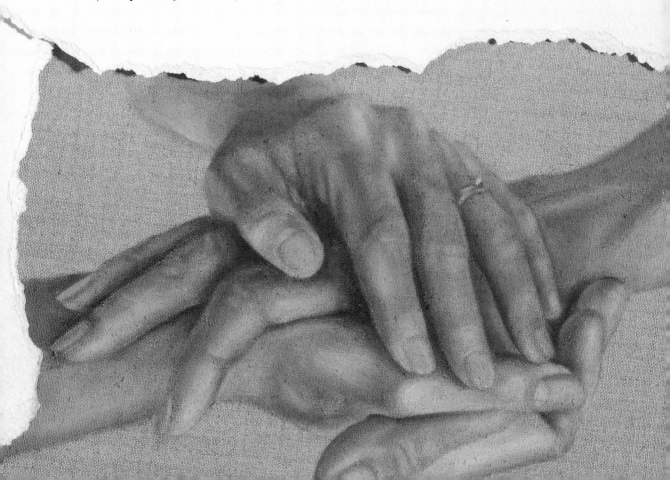

A woman once asked how I envisioned Keith in Heaven. I told her I believed he was busy pointing his mother in the right direction.

To be sure, there are still sad days (though not bad days), and there will always be that nagging feeling that somehow all of this could have been prevented. But I know now that Keith helped me heal. Helped me move from grief to purpose, and from burrowing into self-centeredness to working to prevent similar tragedies.

It was, to a great extent, the precious memories Keith left behind that caused healing. That intense pain in the beginning slowly eased away as we — family and friends — began to realize that sharing those memories filled some of the emptiness still in each of us. So once again, I tell stories of the kid who chased his sisters with a garter snake, farmed with his stepfather and wished upon stars with his mother — my son, whose life saved so many others.

There is a rhythm of the seasons —
planting, growing, harvesting, dying.

It is the rhythm of our lives.

Epilogue

"Nothing raised on the farm is more valuable than children." — *M.A.*

In 1987, a year after the death of her son Keith, Marilyn Adams founded **Farm Safety 4 Just Kids** to educate families about the dangers of flowing grain. Today, it is an international organization whose mission is prevention of farm-related childhood injuries, health risks and fatalities.

Farm Safety 4 Just Kids works to increase public awareness and understanding of the hazards to children on farms, provides people with resources to make farms safer, and motivates them to work for change in safety and health issues. The organization sponsors presentations, workshops and community training. Chapters present school programs, promotional campaigns, family seminars and day camps to learn about farm safety and health. Additionally, **Farm Safety 4 Just Kids** collaborates with government agencies and private organizations concerned with the health and safety of children in all environments.

Prior to the establishment of **Farm Safety 4 Just Kids**, a study by the Harborview Injury Prevention and Research Center in Seattle estimated that 300 children and adolescents were dying each year from farm injuries, and that another 23,500 were suffering non-fatal trauma. An update on that study now indicates that the farm fatality rate for children and adolescents has declined by 39 percent. One can only conclude that **Farm Safety 4 Just Kids** has had a significant impact on the decline. However, the work continues. The study also shows a 10 percent increase in non-fatal farm injuries, demonstrating the need to increase farm safety and health awareness and education.

For more information, contact:
Farm Safety 4 Just Kids
PO Box 458
Earlham, IA USA 50072-0458
Phone: 800-423-KIDS or 515-758-2827
Fax: 515/758-2517
e-mail: fs4jk@netins.net
Web site: http://www.fs4jk.org

Secret Cities

The _ secret cities in this book are scatered all over the universe.

Dear NASA,

I've made blue "Salvage Chopper". glanced at it and sa work, but I decide to take the chan away a career... and see if itll wo might want to

Well, if yo uld do some oth t. All you hav l, ∞, a drawing nt a self ad en velope to.

propulsion lab asadea, Cali.

Please

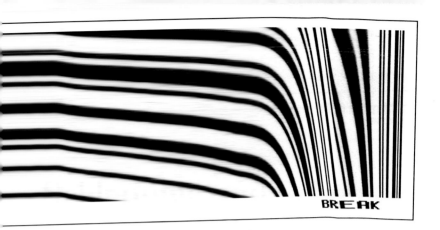

Volume 1:
City of San Diego

By Donald H. Harrison

Cover photos, in clockwise order, from upper left:

Freestanding arch in courtyard of Congregation Beth Am invokes Jewish architecture of Roudnice, Czech Republic, origin of the congregation's Holocaust Torah.
(Photo: Patricia Del Rio, Del Rio Studios).

Holocaust Survivor Ruth Sax and her daughter Sandy Scheller packed the house at the Comic-Con convention of 2018 at the downtown San Diego Convention Center
(Photo: Donald H. Harrison)

The Weinberger Federal Courthouse in downtown San Diego was named for Jacob Weinberger, a Jewish community leader who became the first resident federal judge in San Diego.
(Photo: Donald H. Harrison)

The Aaron S. Gold prayer space, named for one of Tifereth Israel Synagogue's late rabbis, is within the Silverman sanctuary at Tifereth Israel Synagogue. Worshipers enjoy the interplay of sunlight and art during services.
(Photo: gatesphotography.com from Tifereth Israel Synagogue's centennial book, 1905-2005.)

Iconic courtyard of the Salk Institute for Biological Studies was designed by architect Louis Kahn in collaboration with Jonas Salk.
(Photo: Salk Institute)